JUDE DOWNES

Rise of the
Wise Woman

48 Roads to
Self-Discovery

First published 2019

Text copyright © Jude Downes 2019
The moral right of the author has been asserted
Mandala artwork by Irene Charalambidis

All rights reserved. No part of this publication may be reproduced, stored in a retrieval system, or transmitted in any form or by any means, electronic, mechanical, photo-copying, recording or otherwise, without the prior written permission of the publisher and copyright holder.

A self published title designed and produced
by Adala Publishing
www.adalapublishing.com.au

A catalogue record for this book is available from the National Library of Australia

ISBN 978-0-6487116-2-9 (Print)
ISBN 978-0-6487116-3-6 (eBook)
ISBN 978-0-6487116-4-3 (PDF)

www.judedownes.com

Contents

Introduction 1
About Rise of the Wise Woman 5
The Road – A Story 9
How to Work with the Wise Woman 11
The Spreads 15

The Wise Women
  1 Shape Shifter 29
  2 Dream Weaver 31
  3 Seer 33

4	Truth Seeker	35
5	Story Weaver	37
6	Star Traveller	39
7	Healer	41
8	Protector	43
9	Wisdom Keeper	45
10	Earth Mother	47
11	Guardian of the Gate	50
12	Unknown	52
13	Trailblazer	54
14	Spiritual Midwife	56
15	Keeper of Women's Mysteries	58
16	Basket Weaver	60
17	Silent Witness ~ Record Keeper	63
18	Harvest Crone	66
19	Eagle Eyes	69
20	Water Diviner	72
21	Empath	75
22	Warrior	78
23	Quiet Achiever	81
24	Creator	83
25	Grandmother	85
26	Dancer	87
27	Catalyzer	89

28	Keeper of Secrets	91
29	Singer	93
30	Muse	95
31	Caretaker	97
32	Adventurer	99
33	Alchemist	101
34	Observer	103
35	Gardener	105
36	Priestess	108
37	Earth Angel	110
38	Witch	112
39	Gatherer	115
40	Seeker	118
41	Crystal Guardian	121
42	Moon Goddess	124
43	Ceremonial Wise Woman	127
44	Writer	130
45	Elemental Guardian	133
46	Free Spirit	136
47	Keeper of the Flame	139
48	Spirit of the Goddess	142

Ceremony to Invoke the Wise Woman 145

Thank you to my number one supporter, the one who has believed in me since the beginning of our journey together, my wonderful husband Geoffrey. We are a great team!

Introduction

I sit facing the giant red monolith called Uluru in Central Australia. It is 2007 and I am here to participate in ceremony with the Elders. While waiting for ceremony to begin, a friend and I take a little walk. We move off the well-worn track and there is Uluru, standing proud and strong in front of us. A meditative state washes over me as I sit on the warm red earth drinking in the vista.

Closing my eyes, I see the spirit Grandmothers. I feel their innate power as I journey inside the rock. A huge sacred fire several stories high is being tended by the Grandmothers.

Suspended above the fire is a large pink faceted crystal. This crystal turns slowly. As my gaze moves upward, I see the loving energy of this sacred fire. Crystal light flows out the top of Uluru and flows down into the landscape. I am told by the Grandmothers that my work with women will grow and that I am doing the work I am supposed to be doing. Everything I have created is about Divine Feminine empowerment. The meditation was beautiful however I put it aside for a while as I was flying into the busy metropolis of Sydney a few days later.

Arriving into the hustle and bustle of a busy city after the quiet and power of the desert assaults my senses. Everything is jarring my nerves. A woman I'm sharing a room with asks if I would like to visit a new age shop she knows nearby. I answer 'sure, why not.' I need to ground myself into where I am right now.

Entering the shop and feeling the relative peace that comes from such a space, the first thing I notice is a cabinet directly in front of me. Sitting in the bottom of the cabinet, on its own and lit by the light above it is an exact replica, in glass, of the crystal I had seen in my meditation in the desert, including the exact shade of pink.

To me, this is a tangible confirmation of what I am supposed to be doing with my life, empowering women to empower themselves. Of course, the crystal came home with me and it sits next to me as I write or in my workshops to remind me of the loving journey I have agreed to undertake in this lifetime.

Many years pass and I am standing in my own stone circle which is dedicated to the Spirit of the Goddess. It is the dark of the moon and I am setting my intentions for my work with the Wise Woman. Nearby I can hear my owl talking along with me. She has been coming to me in unusual ways for several months, to tell me that the sacred feminine path is my way.

I finish my prayers and she also stops talking. I stand a few moments more in the quiet of the night, waiting, just being present to the moment. I feel her wing brush my hair before I hear three flaps of her wings and she silently moves on into the night.

I have had many confirmations of this sacred path over the years and many challenges as well, but what I would like to say to you dear Wise Woman, is that when you decide to believe in what you are offered as your purpose, back yourself in life and value your worth. Keep putting one foot in front of the other to create what you know in your heart is right for you and those around you.

I love this path I have chosen. Or perhaps it actually chose me. It not only fulfils me; it encourages other women to follow the path they know is right for them.

Another year has passed and over that time I have written about the need for the feminine and the masculine to walk in balance, in Divine Unity, side by side. It is clear that to walk in balance, the Divine Feminine is waking up within men as well. She is a guide for him to assist in the support of bringing balance to our planet. One gender is not more important than the other when they work in harmony. However, woman is showing her vibrancy, her power, her worth as she steps up. The men supporting her are wanting this change in the status quo just as much as she does. They are right there with her, working in their own power and understanding of this new world. It's a brave new world where women and men are finding their balance point. It is being fuelled by love. Although this book was written for the Wise Woman, I encourage men to work with the Wise Woman as his guide to supporting this new world. The Wise Woman shines in us *all*, with love.

Empowering Love

Jude

About the Rise of the Wise Woman

We live in a time where the sacred feminine is rediscovering her voice. She is remembering who she is and what she came here to do. The Wise Woman is awakening in women all over the world, regardless of their chronological age. She is now more visible, more respected and honoured, particularly within herself. The Wise Woman is discovering creative ways to walk in balance with the masculine rather than attempting to swing the pendulum too far the other way.

We live in a changing world and the feminine is raising her voice now, to say, it's time to change the status quo but let's get it right this time.

This book has been created to encourage the rising Wise Woman to recognise that innate core part of herself as she remembers who she is in her power time, as she empowers herself and gives herself permission to discover her purpose in life. This core aspect of self is just one part of her journey, but it offers insight into how she feels within.

Each of the forty-eight roads of self-discovery will touch a remembering part of you as you work with them.

You can choose one initial Wise Woman number for example, which will represent the innate nature of who you are. You can work with any of the Wise Women on a daily basis and choose one for a given situation, or as an answer to a question or guidance for your purpose. You may decide to choose several of the Wise Women archetypes to create a story about your journey and perhaps write the next chapter of your life story.

There are many roads of self-discovery in life. Beyond this Rise of the Wise Woman book you will begin to discover many more roads that fit with your life and where you are heading. Working with a book such as this is just the beginning to empowering yourself to take a chance on life.

Often, all you have to do to begin the journey to remembering who you are, is to open your heart to love and the power of the Wise Woman within.

The Ancient Ones mentioned in the Wise Woman pages are the wise guides of your Ancestral line who have walked these ancient roads before you and who guide you. They encourage women to be the Goddess, the Priestess, the Healer, the Witch, the Gardener, the Story Weaver, and more. All of these are aspects of who you are and are symbolic of the awakening Wise Woman. Each woman will resonate strongly with one or more roads of self-discovery. Enjoy the journey dear Wise Woman, it's a fabulous one!

The Road

A metaphorical story of the Wise Woman
who is remembering her journey.
She is you. You are she.

The road beneath my feet is firm. It's a well-worn path walked by my Ancestors before me. I feel their presence. I hear their laughter. I feel their tears upon my cheeks. I know their challenges, their journey. I feel their love.

My Ancestors, the Ancient Ones call to me to walk this ancient road. I feel the old ones beckoning me, asking me to remember the journey of souls. My ancestral line is ancient, like so many others. Life, love, loss and joy are all part of their journey. It is my own journey now, leaving my personal imprint of experiences as a record of my existence, combining with the records of those who are behind me and all around me. This imprint of souls will be a reminder of the journey for those who will walk this road in the many years ahead.

I walk barefoot. The warm dry earth connects me to my path, my trail, my road through life and the other Wise Women creating change in the world.

I awoke this morning seeing the faces of my Ancestors, the beautiful Ancient Ones. I heard their call, feeling their love across space and time.

These are the Wise Women of times long past. I am of the present. Intuitively I know the time has come to walk this ancient road and take my rightful place as a Wise Woman among all Wise Women remembering the journey of their soul.

My own sacred lineage lines my road. I am the Seer, the Healer, the Story Weaver, the Grandmother and more. The Ancient Ones share with me their wisdom, their learning, their unique journey as the Wise Woman. I remember. I live. I love all who have come before me and all that I am now.

I am … the Wise Woman!

How to work with the Wise Woman

Each road of self-discovery will lead you to understanding a part of yourself. It is a choice to walk that road. Knowledge about self and your journey is power and I see that a road explored is a road well-travelled by the Ancient Ones before us. You are accessing the Wise Woman within you, around you and who she represents to you with her powerful medicine and messages at this time.

Getting to Know your Wise Woman

When you first work with the Rise of the Wise Woman book, it is a good idea to claim the power of your Wise Woman as your own. The more you work with her in her many guises, the more she will grow in your life and the more you will be aware of the Ancient Ones who walk with you, guiding your way.

Each Wise Woman you intuitively choose will hold meaning for you directly from your inner Wise Guide. Read the meaning and what your chosen Wise Woman speaks to you. Words carry a vibration; therefore you may feel warmth spread through you, an understanding might come to you or you may remember that this is who you agreed to be before incarnating into this lifetime. Only then read the message at the bottom of the page.

Each Wise Woman is a gift from the Ancient Ones as you tap into that source of energy to feed you and nourish you from the inside out. It is wisdom about who you came here to be as you understand the journey of the awakened Wise Woman, knowing you are walking the path of remembering the journey.

You will have one Wise Woman, who is the innate part of you, to work with over your lifetime. You will recognise her as the core of who you are. You will also work with many of the other Wise Women in this book to encourage and guide you on your beautiful journey.

Sleep with your new book under your pillow or nearby and say the following:

> 'Dear Ancient Ones of my ancestral line, I am ready to awaken to my own sacred Wise Woman. Guide me well dear Ancient Ones. I am protected on my roads to self-discovery.'

Alternatively, create your own prayer of welcome. In other words, dream her into your life.

This beautiful book is designed as a helpful tool for your journey. However, it is up to you to journey with a loving heart to seek your roads of self-discovery.

The Spreads

I have chosen five ways of working with the Wise Women in these pages, or you may decide to work with them in your own way. The following is a guide only.

The Essence of You

This single Wise Woman choice is about honouring the core of the woman you are remembering. Sit quietly with your book in your hands or against your heart and open your heart and mind to the wisdom coming to you from the Ancient Ones today.

Do this at a time and in a place where you will not be disturbed. Take three deep breaths and release with a sigh. Focus on your breath and allow yourself to slip into a meditative space.

Ask the Ancient Ones to offer you the number of the Wise Woman that most represents the qualities with which you came into this lifetime. Either allow a number between 1 and 48 to come to you through your heart remembering or randomly open the pages until you feel it is time to stop. You could also work with a pendulum to scan down the Wise Woman contents pages to offer you the innate Wise Woman for you.

Trust the wisdom that has chosen you. Turn to the relevant page and read about the Wise Woman and allow her to settle into place as you begin to explore how those qualities have been playing out in your life, in your stories and how those qualities can assist you as you journey forward now.

Where in your body do you feel these qualities? How do they sit with you? How can you work with them now? Once acknowledged, the Ancient Ones will assist you in integrating your new knowledge into your everyday life. You will discover the power of your innate Wise Woman as she works with you in all aspects of your life. She is here to assist you and encourage you to live 'on-purpose', to integrate her wisdom into your everyday life.

Past Present Future

This past, present and future spread is to assist in initiating understanding of the qualities you have brought forward with you from a past life, the qualities you are working with right now as well as your potential future in this lifetime.

When you choose your three Wise Women, you are creating a story to weave into your everyday life.

Ask the Ancient Ones to offer you the three numbers of the Wise Women that most represent the qualities you are working with in this lifetime. Either allow your numbers between 1 and 48 to come to you through your heart remembering or randomly open the pages until you feel it is time to stop. You could also work with a pendulum to scan down the Wise Woman contents pages to discover your past, present and future Wise Women.

Wise Woman One represents your past lives

In one or more past lives you have embodied these qualities. You have chosen this Wise Woman as she is also a part of your journey in this lifetime. Rather than seeing these qualities as something from the past see them as qualities to encourage and empower your journey again in this lifetime.

Wise Woman Two represents your present

You have chosen this Wise Woman to remember the qualities you want or need to work with right now. Your everyday life can be enhanced by recognising these qualities within you.

Wise Woman Three represents your future potential

You have chosen this Wise Woman to encourage you to keep moving, that these qualities are also inherent within you however they are not quite ready for you to work with just yet. This is your future potential.

When you work with the positive vibration and qualities of the Wise Women in one and two, the qualities of Wise Woman number three will be welcomed into your life without fuss when the time is right. You have no need to push anything, as these qualities are a part of you now. You will work with the different energies and roads at different times; however, you will also work with them in unity.

A Road to Follow

Choose one Wise Woman for the day ahead. This is the energy you need in your life right now. This aspect of your

Wise Woman is rising up to be identified and acknowledged for something that is happening in your life. Something that requires the input of this aspect of the Wise Woman. This Wise Woman will assist you on your journey throughout the time she is needed.

You may ask a question or perhaps ask what is needed in your life at this time. Allow the vibration of the Wise Woman to find you simply by trusting your intuition.

Ask the Ancient Ones to offer you the number of the Wise Woman that you most need now. Either allow a number between 1 and 48 to come to you through your heart remembering or randomly open the pages until you feel it is time to stop. You could also work with a pendulum to scan down the Wise Woman contents pages in order to reveal the Wise Woman you need to work with today.

Twelve Month Sacred Circle

Ask the Ancient Ones to guide your choices as you create a story for the twelve months ahead with the strengths of the Wise Woman. As you pass from one month to the next you bring the qualities of the Wise Woman from the previous months with you to build on the story that has begun to grow.

Take a clean sheet of paper and draw a large circle. Draw 12 equal sections. See the example on page 25. I have included a symbol for the triplicity of the Divine Feminine as the core of the twelve-month sacred circle. We honour the wisdom of the Wise Woman as she journeys around the wheel of the year.

Ask the Ancient Ones to offer you the numbers of the Wise Women that you will be working with over the next twelve months. Either allow a number between 1 and 48 to come to you through your heart remembering or randomly open the pages until you feel it is time to stop. You could also work with a pendulum to scan down the Wise Woman contents pages to reveal to you the Wise Women you will work with on your journey. You may also discover that the same Wise Woman vibration will come to you in different months. This twelve month journey doesn't necessarily mean a different Wise Woman in every month. Begin in whichever month suits for the twelve months ahead. Don't wait to begin at the start of the calendar year.

As you choose your Wise Women, begin in the east and move sunwise around the circle, writing a chosen Wise Woman in each of the twelve months of your sacred circle. For example, Shape Shifter in January, Grandmother in September. As you write, you build power with the Wise Woman. There is a deep resonance of the

Divine spark within you. Each Wise Woman offers you an opportunity to grow in your wholeness, to seek out the seeds of light planted so long ago before you incarnated into this physical body.

This is an opportunity to work with your inner Wise Woman as your story is enhanced with the roads of self-discovery you have intuitively chosen.

Create a circle big enough in which to write the twelve Wise Women or work with the circle in this book or the accompanying Wise Women journal. Perhaps your circle is created with crystals, stones, shells or a drawn circle as below. However you choose to create your circle is perfect for you.

The next step is to honour the Wise Women shaping your journey. Place a candle, in a safe receptacle, in a colour of your choice at the centre of your circle to represent the Divine Feminine within you. Allow the Wise Woman for each of the twelve months to come to you, to work with you, to offer you messages and to guide your journey.

As you journey with your chosen Wise Women around the sacred wheel, the central symbol representing your Divine Feminine becomes the key to creating wholeness on your journey.

The symbol of the Divine Feminine is the spark of light that ignites your journey. With this spread you are weaving a story of the potential journey ahead. The messages for each Wise Woman will assist you to know the story of your journey as you integrate them into your everyday life.

Wise Woman Twelve Month Spread

Reading for Another

This Wise Woman quick read will offer immediate guidance. When another woman seeks your guidance, allow her to ask a question. Encourage her to sit quietly as she focuses on her question. She will choose one Wise Woman between 1 and 48. Read the Wise Woman wisdom. Offer her time to absorb the words. Then read the Ancient Ones message at the bottom of the Wise Woman information.

Incorporate the qualities of the Wise Woman as part of her journey to highlight her strengths in moving forward. If further information is needed, repeat the process with another Wise Woman or two, but no more than three.

If you have a client for a healing session or for a reading and would like to make the Wise Women a part of the journey, ask your client to choose a number between 1 and 48 or ask them to randomly open the pages until they feel it is time to stop. You could also work with a pendulum to scan down the Wise Woman contents pages to reveal the Wise Woman to you. Encourage your client to see herself as the Wise Woman and embrace the qualities she chose for her journey.

NOTE: There are many men who will also benefit from accessing their inner sacred Wise Woman or the Divine

Feminine expressed through the Wise Woman. This is a time of walking in balance, in unity, so don't be afraid of working in this way.

The Wise Women

1

Shape Shifter

The Shape Shifter can access different qualities and has the ability to show herself to the world as she wishes to be seen, to affect powerful change where she is guided to assist. She can shift her energy at will once she recognises her shape shifting ability. Her energy body can change to different forms as required.

Astral travel is likely with the Shape Shifter. Lucid dreaming will place the Shape Shifter where she needs to be, as she is also the Observer.

The Shape Shifter can transform into a beautiful Goddess or an ancient hag, simply by focusing on her energy to shift form. Each are needed at different times. The Goddess will become highly visible and recognisable as a force of nature at the forefront of change, and the hag often tends to become invisible. This is the energy of what may be needed at times to work behind the scenes to create change.

The Shape Shifter will immerse herself in many different experiences and adventures. All experiences and adventures lead to creating peace within self and peace around the world.

The Ancient Ones have honoured the Shape Shifter with the ability to either 'blend in' or 'stand out' in her uniqueness.

The Message for Today

If the Shape Shifter has come to you today you are being asked to stand out to make a clear statement in your world. Show yourself as the fabulous Goddess in some way. Stand in your power and allow people to see this Goddess part of you in order to create change in an area of your life. This is a time to create a shift in your personal energy.

2

Dream Weaver

The Dream Weaver is a vivid dreamer. She has the ability to decipher the symbols placed in her dreams by the Ancient Ones. Symbols that honour the road ahead and point out the direction for optimum results.

The Dream Weaver trusts what she is shown. She daydreams as well as dreaming her night-time dreams. Her daydreams are inspired, creating a platform from which to launch her direction.

She can take her dreaming and create a rich tapestry that resembles a map with which to journey through life. She takes the threads of symbols and begins to weave an intricate design, one that includes people, adventures, challenges, and happiness, all created for life's journey. From this place of creation, the Dream Weaver will encourage others who are seeking to weave their own journey into magnificence.

The Dream Weaver will offer clarity in symbolic messages to others when asked.

The Ancient Ones have honoured the Dream Weaver with a unique ability to read the signs and symbols of life in order to create unity and harmony.

The Message for Today

If the Dream Weaver has come to you today you are being asked to look at the symbols of life that are repetitively showing themselves to you. They may arrive in your night-time dreams, daydreams or in everyday life as significant signposts. There are messages inherent within the symbols to guide you on your journey. Pull the symbolic meanings together to create the beginnings of a new life chapter and weave that symbology into your beautiful life tapestry.

3

Seer

The Seer sees beyond the ordinary to the extraordinary. She sees across time and space to what is needed to move the metaphorical mountains of life.

She has the ability to journey beyond the scope of ordinary human consciousness to discover a better path for herself and others.

The Seer will bring back messages from beyond the veil, from loved ones or from guides for direction and healing.

The journeys of the Seer are undertaken with an immense measure of trust.

She sees deeply with her inner vision and her vision in the ordinary world. She has the ability to see beyond what is shown on the surface of life to seek a deeper truth.

When the Seer Wise Woman is invoked she will discover that she is stronger and clearer than at any other time in life.

The Ancient Ones have honoured the Seer with clear vision and a clear voice to express those visions to those who seek her guidance.

The Message for Today

If the Seer has come to you today you are being asked to see beyond your ordinary understanding. There are new ways of journeying to be seen. Meditate, contemplate, walk in nature and look for the signposts that will come to you through your 'seeing'. You have clear vision now. Work with it in powerful and positive ways to bring about change.

4

Truth Seeker

The Truth Seeker holds a strong sense of justice. She will fight for her own rights as well as the rights of others. When the Truth Seeker discovers a worthy cause, she is its champion.

She has the ability to dig deep into her own life to bear witness to her own personal truth and honour it and work with it to help others treading the road as a Truth Seeker.

Understanding that life is never perfect, nor is every situation perfect is an important lesson for the Truth Seeker.

She will always seek truth however she will intuitively know when to keep that truth to herself.

Being a holder of truth can be a hard task-master as secrets will inevitably show themselves to the Truth Seeker. Understanding that these sometimes need to be metaphorically buried in the earth is important to note. Not all secrets need to be shared, in fact it may be harmful to do so.

The Truth Seeker will not remain silent to injustice. She stands strong, shoulder to shoulder with other Wise Women, to right the wrongs in the world.

The Ancient Ones have honoured the Truth Seeker with a true heart and voice to stand in advocacy for those who have no voice or for those who speak but are not heard.

The Message for Today

If the Truth Seeker has come to you today, a secret is becoming known. It may be yours to share or it is someone close to you who wants to share with you. The Truth Seeker will guide you to discover what is truth and what are false memories. By being able to differentiate the truth from falsehoods, the secret revealed can no longer hold power over you or someone you love unless you allow it.

5

Story Weaver

The Story Weaver holds a wealth of stories within her heart and soul. She is the one who has the ability to tell them well.

She has held her stories close to her until the right time arrived to begin sharing them. It is through her story weaving that others will learn and grow. Sitting at the kitchen table over a cup of tea or perhaps in nature sitting under an ancient tree, she will share her stories with others who are willing to listen and learn, as well as with other Story Weavers.

Her creative spirit will write the book of wisdom for others to follow in her steps. She never chastises, rather she allows others to follow if they wish to learn from her experiences or they may choose to walk away. The Story Weaver speaks her truth from the heart. She never seeks approval for her stories. They are there as teaching tools if others are willing to learn from them.

The Story Weaver has a lifetime of powerful stories to share, to honour those coming along behind her who wish to seek knowledge and wisdom about life's journey.

The Ancient Ones have honoured the Story Weaver with many life adventures so that she may encourage others on their quest for adventure.

The Message for Today

If the Story Weaver has come to you today there is a need to gather with family and friends to share stories about the past, the present and the dreams for the future. It is time to learn about your history, about the ones who came before you. It is time to create new chapters in your own life story that will be handed down and heard by the ones who come after you. The keys to your future lay within the seeds of the past and the present.

6

Star Traveller

The Star Traveller looks into the inky starlit night sky for her inspiration. She speaks of the star people, of home. She speaks of planetary alignments, eclipses and the Alchemy of the Spirit.

She knows she has a purpose on this great earth and yet, at times, she feels alone until she finds another Star Traveller who shares that unique path.

Her way in the world has always been unique and never quite fits in with plans others have for the planet. She sees beyond the ordinary to what is truly possible and yet, at times, lacks the know-how to implement that knowledge. Times are changing as the Star Traveller activates her inner knowledge that directs her to where she needs to be, doing what needs to be done.

To assist others who feel the same as she does is important. Her journey is to bring together others of like mind to hold the energy of the stars on earth.

The Star Traveller seeks her inner wisdom, knowing it comes from beyond this earthly realm.

The Ancient Ones have honoured the Star Traveller with the gift of reaching for the stars, for seeing beyond this earthly life to worlds unknown in an ordinary sense.

The Message for Today

If the Star Traveller has come to you today take some time to look up at the stars. It is time to be inspired beyond what you see in the everyday world. It is time perhaps, to write the next chapter in your book of life. You are ready for change.

7

Healer

The Healer holds in her hands and her heart a sacred gift of healing light. She has long known of her healing abilities. Now is her time to step further into her role as a powerful healer.

She knows that the soul of each person is capable of healing anything and her role is as a catalyzer for that healing to occur.

The Healer will offer many different ways of healing as she gathers her healing tools around her. She knows that these symbols of healing are important to the journey, but true healing occurs through powerful intention, along with the voices of the ancient spirit healers speaking with the soul to create a healing journey.

The true healer is wise and compassionate with an innate knowing of what needs healing. She offers her healing to this great earth. She aids in the journey to forgiveness for the pain inflicted by humanity.

The Healer is at home with her healing capabilities. Sometimes it is through her hands, often it is through her words.

The Ancient Ones have honoured the Healer with the gift of healing the spirit of those who seek her and to help them discover their own unique healing journey.

The Message for Today

If the Healer has come to you today you are being asked to heal something that is old and no longer needed in your life; an old story. This is a time to create a healed sacred inner space within your life in order to seed something new and exciting.

8

Protector

The Protector is fierce as she protects all that she loves. She is also a force to be reckoned with as she stands in her own power. As a Protector she has learned to say no and mean it.

Her many years of experience have shown the Protector what she will and will not tolerate in her life. Speaking out will often make others feel uncomfortable, however their reactions are none of her business.

Change for the Protector will only come when she speaks out and takes action. Nothing as important as saving lives, species, and the environment escapes her notice. She has nothing to lose in her protection and those around her have everything to gain. She can be rash in rushing forward and needs to sometimes consider the consequences of her actions and words carefully. There are ways of expression and on occasion a considered approach works its magic best.

The Protector looks out for those who are bullied and persecuted. She protects the environment, writes letters, attends protests, and speaks out about violence against women, children, the elderly and infirm.

The Ancient Ones have honoured the Protector with the dual gifts of strength and courage. They encourage her to stand tall in her beliefs and the rights and beliefs of others.

The Message for Today

If the Protector has come to you today it is time to protect that which is sacred to you and release anything that interferes with your journey. New journeys and new ideas await. For now, keep the energy of them close to you until it is time to reveal them to a greater world.

9

Wisdom Keeper

The innate wisdom of the Wisdom Keeper reaches out in every direction.

She receives her wisdom from all aspects of nature and through her own adventures. Wisdom is something she has grown to embrace. She has an instinctive knowing of the right things to be expressed at the right time.

Often, the Wisdom Keeper knows her wisdom without knowing how she knows. She knows who will listen and who is not willing to hear the wisdom of the earth and stars. She is discerning about those with whom she shares her wisdom. The Wisdom Keeper does not suffer fools. She will be polite, however, unless it feels right and she feels safe to express her wisdom, she will keep it to herself.

The Wisdom Keeper only offers her wisdom when sought rather than expressing it to all who will listen. She keeps her wise counsel close until it is truly needed.

The Ancient Ones have honoured the Wisdom Keeper with the gift of seeking true wisdom from the Goddess and the Stars and through her own experiences. She is here to guide, support and share so that others too may find their way.

The Message for Today

If the Wisdom Keeper has come to you today it is time to share some of the wisdom you hold deep within you with those who are prepared to listen. You will know if the wisdom is for you alone or if it is something to be shared. Listen to your own wise counsel first.

10

Earth Mother

The Earth Mother is deeply connected to this beautiful planet and feels what Mother Earth feels in her joy, her pain and sorrow. She feels her power, her strength and her courage. The Earth Mother knows her greater purpose involves being at one with the Earth and listening to her messages.

The Earth Mother is family oriented and loves nothing more than nurturing those around her. She is often the Matriarch. She is a woman to be seen and honoured for her earthly advice.

She is gentle, yet powerful and more often than not she is willing to take life in her stride. When her world is rocked by chaos, she has the ability to pick up the pieces and know the way forward, just like Mother Earth. The Earth Mother is the keeper of historical events. She is also the creator of beauty in a practical earthly way. She never seeks approval because she does not need it. She just is—the Earth Mother.

The Earth Mother accepts her role with humility and love. She steps into her role with a natural ability to take charge whilst making others feel comfortable in their own roles within a family unit and society. This role is as natural as breathing to her.

The Ancient Ones have honoured the Earth Mother with the gift of nurturing. Self-nurturing is also important so that she may nurture others in this same manner. To live a balanced life on earth, we must have nurturing Earth Mothers to help us survive and thrive on our journey.

The Message for Today

If the Earth Mother has come to you today it is time to nurture yourself. You are in need of some soul nourishment, some time out that is just for you. You can only nourish others when you yourself have been nourished. Offer yourself the gift of time and reconnect with the energy of Mother Earth.

11

Guardian of the Gate

The Guardian of the Gate is a gatekeeper who will nourish those souls ready to cross the threshold of what we call physical death, or transition. This important role will also guide those who are ready to release the old painful stories that have held them back from creating the life they desire.

The Guardian of the Gate is strong and courageous as she sees beyond the veil to who is waiting for those ready to transition into a new form. She holds the gate open and acts as a guide, to show the beauty of the realm beyond the ordinary world they are leaving behind.

As Guardian of the Gate, she has the ability to walk between worlds, helping those who require her assistance. She listens with her heart and soul, rather than her physicality, to the calls of those who need her.

The Guardian of the Gate accepts her role as a gatekeeper of the journey of the soul. She also holds the dual role of birthing new souls into this world, as well as gatekeeper for departing souls. Her journey is a full one.

The Ancient Ones have honoured the Guardian of the Gate with strength to take on such an important role at the beginning of human life and at the end in death, to begin the cycle once more.

The Message for Today

If the Guardian of the Gate has come to you today there may be someone from beyond the veil trying to get in touch with you. Notice the signs around you and get a feel for who it is. A message for you or someone you love is waiting to be heard.

12

Unknown

The Unknown, as the name suggests, is a mystery. She does not fit into any particular role. She has the ability to be invisible when needed and highly visible when it is necessary. The Unknown is like a chameleon and will fit in wherever she is.

She is all things and can choose her role to suit the moment. Her wisdom runs deep, her nurturing skills are beautiful. She is Protector, Wise Woman, Shape Shifter and more and yet she is also none of these things. Her journey in these years is beyond the scope of ordinary understanding. The Unknown can be secretive at times, not even she knows what is to be achieved until it becomes clear to her in just the right moment. Her thoughts and feelings appear to be beyond the normal human capacity for knowing.

The Unknown will complete many tasks that aid humanity without others knowing what she has achieved. She accepts that accolades are not hers to take as she quietly goes about making a difference in her world, which ultimately affects the greater world.

The Ancient Ones have honoured the Unknown with courage to make a difference in quiet and unassuming ways. They have charged her with creating sacred space for healing and wellbeing for the planet and for her inhabitants, without the general knowledge of the human race. Hers is a quieter, seemingly unassuming journey.

The Message for Today

If the Unknown has come to you today, be open to messages coming to you about the journey ahead. The messages for your journey will come in a variety of ways. Today is one of trusting your journey.

13

Trailblazer

The Trailblazer is one who comes out with energetic guns blazing to make a difference in the world. She is a pioneer who thinks and feels outside the metaphorical ordinary box. She knows the way forward and is often thwarted in her endeavours to make a difference and yet she never gives up. She is a forward thinker who can see into the future about how something will play out if certain steps are taken, to arrive at the best destination and with the assistance of the right equipment for the journey; her sacred tools.

She knows she needs to be seen because her path as the Trailblazer is a big one, whether it is within the context of her family, local community or a greater world stage.

The Trailblazer will know how to travel her well-forged path. Even in the face of adversity she will know how to implement change in her own life first, before letting it flow into her community and the greater world.

The Ancient Ones have honoured the Trailblazer with a knowing of her true path. She is charged with speaking from her heart and knowing that it is right. Her path is to change something important in her world and thus influence the greater world.

The Message for Today

If the Trailblazer has come to you today you are being asked to forge a new path, write a new chapter in your book of life. You will think about something differently in the days ahead that may take you on a different journey to the one you thought you were travelling. Exciting times are coming your way.

14

Spiritual Midwife

The Spiritual Midwife offers birthing support to those who are ready to birth their ideas, dreams and goals into the world.

She is the 'go-to' woman when knowledge and wisdom are needed in the planning stages prior to new birth and to be there through the subsequent labour and birth.

The Spiritual Midwife is the mentor, counsellor, nurturer, tough love component of an ancient birthing process that assists mind, body, soul and emotions on their journey to new life in a holistic way.

When she is called, she knows her place is by the side of the one giving birth. There is no jealousy or envy by the Spiritual Midwife for another's journey. There is sincere joy for the recognition that something fabulous is being birthed into the world and pride in knowing that her unconditional support helped smooth the way for ease of birth.

The Spiritual Midwife is aware that her role is a supportive one, to help and guide new and positive birth to the planet.

The Ancient Ones have honoured the Spiritual Midwife with the gift of unconditional support of the ideas, dreams and goals of others. All great births require great birthing support.

The Message for Today

If the Spiritual Midwife has come to you today you are being asked to get ready to birth something new into your life. This birth will be something 'value-added' to your journey by adding to the wise collection of sacred tools with which you currently weave your magic in the world.

15

Keeper of Women's Mysteries

The Keeper of Women's Mysteries is a deeply sacred feminine advocate for change and acceptance.

She feels the pain of the earth and of woman deeply as she seeks ways to heal, so often by healing herself first. Women's mysteries are held deep within the heart and soul of the Goddess, Mother Earth and in the stars.

The Keeper of Women's Mysteries heart aches with injustices and an unbalanced society. She needs space and nature to recharge. She is a beacon of light in a dark storm for others who seek her wisdom.

The Keeper of Women's Mysteries is the one who will teach from her heart with wisdom rather than knowledge gained through others. She finds solace in nature when the weeping of the world gets too much for her. Her journey is a big one in this time of the rise of the sacred feminine.

Mother Earth, the Goddess, is her teacher, mentor, healer, balancer, sharer of sacred wisdom.

The Keeper of Women's Mysteries is gentle and yet strong. She knows and feels the pain of the Earth and humanity. She shares her wise counsel with love.

The Ancient Ones have honoured the Keeper of Women's Mysteries with the gift of love for a better world through remembering ancient times, and the mysteries of who woman really is in a world of patriarchy.

The Message for Today

If the Keeper of Women's Mysteries has come to you today you are being asked to begin a spiritual quest for knowledge and wisdom and share what you learn with others. It may be a meditation group or something more profound. You will know how much you are willing to share and with whom.

16

Basket Weaver

The Basket Weaver is sacred to the journey of woman. Although for some, the metaphorical basket they have worked with in their Maiden and Mothering years feels a little worn out because of the constant filling with Goddess energy and then emptying as life lessons spilled over it. The basket is still strong and holds a great deal of creative spirit and the wisdom of many years' experience.

The Basket Weaver's journey is one of empowering others so that they may repair any damage to their sacred basket (a representation of the womb), whilst also knowing that it has found its perfect shape in life.

The Basket Weaver also teaches women how to weave a new basket on life's journey and fill it up in different ways. She is often a craftswoman who shares stories through the art of basket weaving or other craft pursuits. The stories of life are woven into the strands of grass and wicker as she works with women to create a holder of beauty, wisdom and creation.

The old basket and the new basket become one on the journey of life.

The Basket Weaver is aware of her gentle nature. She shares her stories and wisdom through her creative spirit.

The Ancient Ones have honoured the Basket Weaver with the gift of creation through her hands and her soft words. Many will find the journey of creating something tangible, a powerful healing journey.

The Message for Today

If the Basket Weaver has come to you today you are being asked to show others how to repair their own sacred baskets. You are also being asked to repair your own. Life may have been a little rough and the time to regroup and repair with others of similar heart is necessary. A strong basket will hold a great deal of strength, courage and wisdom.

17

Silent Witness ~ Record Keeper

The Silent Witness ~ Record Keeper bears witness to the sufferings and triumphs of humanity. Her role is to bear sacred witness to what is happening on earth. Being a witness is honouring the truth of the reality of what happens in this physical realm and what happens in the spirit realms, as one supports the other.

The role of Silent Witness ~ Record Keeper is not to communicate what she is witnessing in this physical world but rather to record what she sees and knows in the history books of the Universal Records. There is a profound sense of responsibility in accurately recording what the eyes and ears offer in this world.

This beautiful Wise Woman will see and experience much that is beyond the scope of ordinary understanding. She knows the reality of what she is witnessing rather than what appears on the surface of life. She holds an understanding of the workings of the greater Universe.

The Silent Witness ~ Record Keeper knows the greater destiny of humanity. Perhaps not consciously, but she has access to greater records than most.

The Ancient Ones have honoured the Silent Witness ~ Record Keeper with the gift of clear seeing and clear hearing so that she may record accurately the events of humanity, and this great earth, as they attempt to coexist and grow together.

The Message for Today

If the Silent Witness ~ Record Keeper has come to you today you are being asked to keep your spiritual eyes and ears open as well as your physical senses as events are unfolding about which you need to be mindful. Be aware of the detail around you so that you can record what you are witnessing. Things may not be as they appear on the surface, so look deeply by connecting with the bigger picture and see things as they really are.

18

Harvest

The Harvest has a symbolic cornucopia of the fruits of her labours to share with those who seek her out. Her abundance for all of life's precious gifts shines from the core of her being. She has learned a lot in her life about how to get the best out of life events.

She is always available to share not only her abundant wisdom, but her abundance of love and joy as well. She shares abundance from her own vegetable garden and fruit trees. Her role is one of sharing, a little or a lot. It is natural for the Wise Woman of the Harvest to share.

If the Harvest woman has an excess of something, she will quietly seek out those who need a little extra assistance in some area of their life. She is clever and has the ability to put others at ease. She has no need to wait until others ask for her help as she knows just how difficult that is for many. She is the quiet observer. She knows who requires help and sets about making it happen.

The Harvest woman understands that her journey is one of sharing, with loving intent, her abundance with those who need a helping hand.

The Ancient Ones have honoured the Harvest woman with the gift of recognising that even in the darkest of times there is abundance to share. At times throughout the life of the Harvest woman, there will be a lot or a little but her willing heart will always be prepared to share something of importance that will make a difference in the lives of those with whom she shares.

The Message for Today

If the Harvest woman has come to you today it is time to share something with someone who needs your assistance.

It may be physical assistance that is required, such as helping someone pack up their possessions. It may be that you need to offer some wise words to help someone who cannot see the way forward, or perhaps someone needs your abundant love to be expressed today.

19

Eagle Eyes

Eagle Eyes sees the bigger picture of life. She has a way of seeing what needs to be done and sets about doing it, encouraging others to also see the big picture. Others sometimes do not see her vision and try and knock it to the ground. She is someone who is often ahead of her time and can see when others do not. Eagle Eyes vision is often coded with deep symbolic representations that need to be explored in order to unravel their true meaning. This makes her messages all the more profound.

Eagle Eyes will have a goal, a dream. When she takes off to fly on the currents of life through her dreams and meditations, she flies higher and higher. Her vision is clear and sharp, her eyes always on the goal. She sees not just her goal, her dream, she sees what is around it that will help her achieve her destiny and fulfilment of the goal. She will also see the things that will challenge her along the way to success.

She has the ability to lift others up on their journey to see the bigger picture of their life and to see what is affecting their own journey in profound ways. The view from this perspective adds a new dimension to her Wise Woman spirit.

Eagle Eyes often works in conjunction with the Seer and together, whether it is with another Wise Woman or two aspects of the same Wise Woman, prophecy becomes a big part of the journey.

Eagle Eyes takes what she sees, often in symbolic ways and translates the messages into understandable directives for the greater community.

The Ancient Ones have honoured Eagle Eyes with the gift of seeing the symbolic messages of life from a higher perspective. They have given her the voice to share what she sees with those who seek her wisdom.

The Message for Today

If Eagle Eyes has come to you today it is time to take a journey into the higher realms and see something from that higher perspective. It is time to look beyond what appears to be happening in the everyday world and grasp the symbols that will lead you and others forward. As you retrain your mind and heart to interpret the symbols that come to you, you will discover the profound direction in which to head, or encourage others on their journey.

20

Water Diviner

The Water Diviner is drawn to all different types of water bodies. She is influenced by the moon's energies and feels the pull of the moon deeply. She loves the tranquil streams, the raging rivers, the might of the ocean and the glorious majesty of a waterfall.

She has the ability to see into water for messages and healing. The Water Diviner sees the emotions of the world, she sees truth in the shimmering surface of water, even when others cannot see it for themselves.

She is drawn to mermaids and whales, dolphins and other creatures of water. She longs to swim with them, to explore the depths of the watery ways. The Water Diviner has the ability to discover water in the most parched of lands and this is also metaphorical for discovering inner messages for others through the gift of water. The human body is, on average, made up of 60% water, therefore the Water Diviner will work with others through water divination for healing and messages. She connects with the water spirits.

She is the emotional giver of healing through water. Sacred tears are her way of expressing release of emotional wounds.

The Water Diviner looks deeply into the lives and events of others who seek her watery divination ways. She offers support, comfort and direction for the path ahead.

The Ancient Ones have honoured the Water Diviner with the gift of healing the emotional wounds of those who seek her out. She also has the gift of energetically healing the waterways of the world to keep them clear of old emotional debris and the releasing of stagnant energy.

The Message for Today

If the Water Diviner has come to you today you are being asked to look into the emotional waters of life to understand what or who requires your healing words and ways. It may be your own emotional healing that needs examining right now or perhaps someone close to you is reaching out for guidance. Find a place in nature to sit where you can be with the water element and immerse yourself meditatively in the watery beauty to ask for guidance for the way forward.

21

Empath

The Empath feels *everything* deeply. Her journey can be a difficult one when she feels the pain of the world around her. However, the Empath has the ability to feel what is happening within someone or with Mother Earth, often before something happens.

She is a woman of deep feeling and experience. When she understands her journey as an Empath and works with it to guide others on their journey then she will help heal the world as it moves through transitory times.

The Empath knows her journey is a feeling and experiencing one and many times it brings her to her knees. She has learned a lot about how to work with her empathic nature to bring about change in a pain-stricken world. She copes with her depth of feeling by connecting with Mother Earth to release all she feels into the earth to be healed and returned to her as wisdom and healing light.

The Empath knows her path can often be overwhelming with her depth of feeling and knowing and yet she knows that it is her journey to assist those who need her wisdom. Once shared, the pain of that feeling is released.

The Ancient Ones have honoured the Empath with the gift of feeling deeply the wounds of those who walk this earth and Mother Earth herself. They know that it may not feel like a gift but those who feel to this depth often make the best healers.

The Message for Today

If the Empath has come to you today it is a time of deep feeling and expression. If you find yourself doing something 'out of the ordinary' that doesn't seem like you, take a step back and see if you have taken on someone else's personality or baggage. It is important today to discern and take ownership of your life, and release what you may have picked up from someone else.

22

Warrior

The Warrior is prepared to battle anyone or anything that harms another or silences the minorities of this world. Her energy is strong as a protector of the innocent.

She is also a Warrior who protects landscapes as she feels the pain of Mother Earth deep within, as humanity seeks to destroy her beauty.

The Warrior will do more than sign petitions. She will actively engage in verbal communication with governments and corporations to bring about lasting change. Her words are strong and her heart is courageous. She holds no fear of retribution. The Warrior marches to her own beat when she knows that others need her strong voice to go in to bat for them.

The Warrior embodies the Truth Seeker and the Protector as well as her own unique powers of persuasion. She is a leader gifted with the power of the spoken and written word to make her point.

The Warrior does not bother with the negative words flung at her by others who seek to belittle and tarnish her reputation and label her as a troublemaker. She still marches resolutely forward to encourage others to have the powerful voice of the Warrior.

The Warrior is aware of her strengths and works with them to bring about social justice in a world where many declare it is too big a problem to solve.

The Ancient Ones have honoured the Warrior with the gift of strength and gentle power. They know her journey is one of bringing transformative and positive change into a jaded world where there is a deep need for transformation in gentle and powerfully persuasive ways in order to achieve profound results.

The Message for Today

If the Warrior has come to you today there is a need for you to right the wrongs of an injustice in an area of your life. This is a time for you to voice your knowledge and set the record straight. There may also be a situation that requires your intervention and to lend your voice to a worthy cause, either locally or globally.

23

Quiet Achiever

The Quiet Achiever walks gently in the world doing good deeds, often without the knowledge of others. She is a giver of time and energy. Her journey is one of knowing her own worth without seeking it outside of herself. She has no need of validation.

Seeing the smile of others when they discover something special—a gift, a need, a bill paid anonymously perhaps—are all the validation she needs. Often, she does not know the end result of her Quiet Achiever spirit.

The Quiet Achiever will go out of her way to comfort in ways others are so often not aware of and yet, when others do see her good deeds she is quick to brush their importance aside preferring to see relief or joy on the faces of those she has helped in some way.

The Quiet Achiever is aware that her strengths lie in her need for anonymity to do the good work she knows is her role on life's journey.

The Ancient Ones have honoured the Quiet Achiever with the gift of unconditional love for those who seek her out and the gift of identifying her unique ability to know who needs her quiet assistance.

The Message for Today

If the Quiet Achiever has come to you today you are being asked to look around you to see how you can help yourself or another. Often the Quiet Achiever needs to begin by helping herself before she can suitably help others. Today marks a beginning on your journey in some way to making a quiet difference in your world and perhaps in the world of someone close to you.

24

Creator

The Creator is a whirlwind of creative energy. She often sees something special in the world long before others can. She might be an artist, an author, a chef, a gardener, a weaver, a singer or a storyteller. Her journey is one of sharing her knowledge and wisdom of the creative world.

She will encourage others on their journey in life through the creative spirit. The realm of the imagination is her world. It is vibrant and alive with possibilities.

The everyday world will be enriched through a powerful and enlivened creative journey.

The Creator is full of life and colour. She offers wisdom through the creative journeys of life.

The Creator knows that her creations will reach out into the world to bring love, laughter and vibrancy to an ordinary life.

The Ancient Ones have honoured the Creator with the gift of a colourful personality and a vibrant creative gift to share with those who wish to learn the ways of creation through play.

The Message for Today

If the Creator has come to you today you are being asked to play in a creative way. Imagination is the key to your creative explorations. What you imagine creatively can awaken a path of new exploration and potentially open the door for new opportunities to enter. Be vibrant, express yourself in creative ways. See with new creative vision and you might just see something old with fresh eyes.

25

Grandmother

The Grandmother holds the wisdom of life experience. Her eyes twinkle with mischief and irreverence for life's rules. She is courageous in the face of adversity and holds a distinctive 'don't mess with me' attitude when challenged.

She is the keeper of life events that have helped shape her world. She is the keeper of her own story, to be shared with the generations coming after her.

The Grandmother has a deep love for humanity and nature. She loves to nourish and hold those who need her close to her heart.

The Grandmother is no longer the archetypal stooped white-haired old woman. She is vibrant and in her time of sacred feminine power. She is the Keeper of the Wise Blood.

The Grandmother is honoured for her many years on this earth.

The Ancient Ones have honoured the Grandmother with the gifts of nurturance and feminine wisdom that come from living her life in a full and complete way.

The Message for Today

If the Grandmother has come to you today you are being asked to nurture yourself first with a gift of healing or doing something that is nourishing to your body, mind and soul. When you heal and nurture self first, you will then have so much more to offer another. Others reflect what you yourself need, so that you walk your walk, and talk your talk with your Grandmother wisdom.

26

Dancer

The Dancer is one who sees the beauty in life through the dance and movement of the Earth and of all things in nature as they entwine and connect with each other through the joy of spiritual dance.

She is the Wise Woman who dances through life offering her lovely creative spirit to a wide audience. The Dancer will whirl and twirl around others to show the nature of dancing in beauty with life. Sometimes likened to fairy energy she is light on her feet, teaching others how to dance their way to new beginnings with every turn.

She is the wind journeying with the will of delight. Her way is to teach others how to play and laugh.

The Dancer knows she will dance her way into the hearts of those who need to discover a lighter way forward.

The Ancient Ones have honoured the Dancer with the gifts of light-hearted joy and pleasure with the ability to bring those qualities to those who seek her.

The Message for Today

If the Dancer has come to you today you are being asked to feel the freedom of your spirit. You are being asked to ignite within you a passion for life, that comes to you as you dance. Feel your light, because today you dance with the spirit of life.

27

Catalyzer

The Catalyzer is the creator of change in a way that invites others to follow her because they believe in her. She speaks a truth that others recognise within their heart and soul. A Catalyzer is passionate about change when she sees something isn't working.

The Catalyzer is often a wonderful orator, sharing her strategies for change with those who also seek reform of some sort. She is a leader who will gather together a band of people who think the same way, but need a leader to pull it all together.

She is the voice of sound reason in an often chaotic time.

The Catalyzer has the ability to understand instantly what needs to be done and sets about putting strategies in place to create the needed change in a given situation.

The Ancient Ones have honoured the Catalyzer with the gifts of organisation and speaking out. She will create social change in times that need new and fresh ideas and ideals.

The Message for Today

If the Catalyzer has come to you today you are being asked to see with your inner vision what it is that requires change around you. Take the time to look at your organisational skills to seek answers for implementing change in big, or not so big ways.

28
Keeper of Secrets

The Keeper of Secrets is one who listens, often to what is not being said rather than what is being said. She has the ability to listen with her heart to the secrets of others. She also listens to the secrets of the world and the Universe. She knows the secrets of wisdom. She knows the lies perpetuated through an ancestral line.

The Keeper of Secrets holds all secrets to her so that she may know where to place her energy to help another. She does not share the secrets she holds for that becomes gossip. She has the ability to quietly walk where others do not dare, due to harsh judgement. She is aware of the backstory to the journeys of others and she holds them sacred.

Her knowledge offers her the opportunity to discover what will help others without giving away their secrets. Knowing the secrets of the world and the Universe also provides her with sacred tools with which to weave her magic. She will also work with the Keeper of Mysteries, the Seer and the Catalyzer Wise Women to bring about change. Others trust her to keep their stories sacred and safe.

The Keeper of Secrets knows who needs her listening ear.

The Ancient Ones have honoured the Keeper of Secrets with the gifts of sacred sight and understanding so that she may know what needs to be known for the greater good.

The Message for Today

If the Keeper of Secrets has come to you today you are being asked to see beyond the ordinary and reach into a world where the secrets of the Universe are known. There are secrets hidden from others that will become known to you. The secrets revealed will guide your way forward.

29

Singer

The Singer is the storyteller in song. Her voice is her gift. Whether reciting poetry, creating spell work, singing a favourite song or writing a lilting ballad for others, her way is part song bird, part storyteller. She sings with her heart.

The Singer sings over the bones of her Ancestors, weaving her sacred stories over millennia into her favourite songs. A song for every journey is the way of the Singer. She may be called to sing for the wellbeing of the earth or for an individual or situation. As the Singer, she is gifted with words in a prayerful way.

She is a creatrix, a Wise Woman with a gift for sharing stories that others will listen to and understand their beautiful inherent meaning; sacred keys hidden in the words and music.

The Singer is known for wisdom that is offered through her voice. A hypnotic quality that soothes the soul and heart.

The Ancient Ones have honoured the Singer with the gift of a beautiful voice, whether it is the spoken word in meditation or a beautiful song with music. The listener will experience a shift in her perception as she discovers the keys for life that will carry her forward.

The Message for Today

If the Singer has come to you today you are being asked to create a new song to sing. It may be that the earth is calling to you now to sing to her, to create healing within the song you will sing in your prayers.

30

Muse

The Muse is the one who inspires others on their creative journey. She is the Wise Woman who knows the creative spirit intimately. She is positive and inspirational and may often be found as a motivational speaker. Her passion for helping others will be a guiding light for many.

This sacred Wise Woman is fully aware that inspiration is her way. Others are inspired by her just by being in her presence. She loves nothing more than to see the people around her smile and feel love as they create ideas, dreams and goals.

She is practical in her inspiration, knowing that with the heralding of the creative spirit there needs to be practical knowledge on how to achieve their creativity once it is ignited.

The Muse role is one of inspiring others to be the best version of their creative selves they can be.

The Ancient Ones have honoured the Muse with the gift of inspiration to create. They have honoured her with a beauty that emerges from deep within her soul, a beauty that touches all with whom she comes into contact. So often it is without them knowing why they feel inspired.

The Message for Today

If the Muse has come to you today you are being asked to smile and show the world your inner beauty. This smile will ignite the creative spirit in someone today simply by being the delightful and inspiring woman you are. No words are needed right now.

31

Caretaker

The Caretaker is the woman who looks out for others and does her best to keep them safe. She is often a teacher in many different fields. She establishes her authority early on in life and it grows over the many years she lives this life. Even when she retires from her chosen profession she will continue her Caretaker role.

The Caretaker is a nourisher in this physical world. She is the one who will bake you a cake and offer a cuppa and a listening ear. She is the one who is first to volunteer when something needs to be done. The Caretaker is one who will inherently look after our great earth.

She is stronger than she looks. Sometimes overlooked in favour of her Warrior or her Grandmother sisters, the Caretaker needs to stand firm and quietly go about her business, showing her strength by action rather than words. The Caretaker role is one of taking care of people or a situation. She is usually part of a group of other Caretakers.

The Caretaker knows her path is one of looking after others or the earth. She will know what needs to be done when the call for earthly nourishment comes to her heart.

The Ancient Ones have honoured the Caretaker with the gift of being at the forefront of caring for someone or something. She is often gifted and charged with caretaking Mother Earth.

The Message for Today

If the Caretaker has come to you today you are being asked to nourish yourself first and then seek out someone who needs your care. It might be as simple as sharing a meal with someone or it may be something bigger and deeper. You will know what needs to be done because you are the Caretaker.

32

Adventurer

The Adventurer is the woman who seeks the heights of what is available as she explores her world. She will be someone who loves to travel even if it is only in her imagination. She can explore everything from the highest mountains to the deepest valleys, or out into the galaxies.

The Adventurer has a need to know. Her natural curiosity about life, the world and the Universe will see others who have a thirst to know, seek her. This also makes her a great storyteller.

She is wise about the things that interest her and she is willing to share what she knows and understands about the greater world. She is exceptional with her grasp of the big and small scenarios of the world. She has the ability to apply what she witnesses in nature to her everyday world.

The Adventurer knows her journey is one of taking others along on her adventures. Many will seek her knowledge and wisdom through curiosity and will ultimately develop a deeper understanding of themselves along the way. She will challenge those who seek her company to be the best version of themselves they can be.

The Ancient Ones have honoured the Adventurer with the gift of knowing how far to journey to help others find their own adventure. She will know what metaphors to draw from nature to use on each adventure.

The Message for Today

If the Adventurer has come to you today you are being asked to seek your next adventure. Look around you and see who is excited for you and who wants to journey with you. You come together as a match for new discoveries on life's adventures.

33

Alchemist

The Alchemist has the ability to change something basic into something beautiful. As the Alchemist, the Wise Woman will show others how to heal through transforming energies. She is vigilant, adaptive and sees the ways of the individuals who require her help. She knows that no two journeys are the same. She knows that others have the ability to transform energy in their life by working with their fears and doubts and learning how to transform them into something that will take them forward on their journey.

The Alchemist is also the Seer. A woman who will see deep within others to the heart of what gifts they hold sacred. She sees the golden potential within others in order to work with them for their highest and best outcome. She understands what can be changed and what can be worked with to affect positive powerful transformation.

The Alchemist will draw out the stories of others to guide them to a place of personal empowerment. Her way is take the base story and encourage them to discover the sacred keys to transformation held within that story.

The Alchemist knows her way is to encourage others to seek the next transforming cycle on their journey to fulfilment.

The Ancient Ones have honoured the Alchemist with the gift of transforming the stories of others into the keys for healing and empowerment.

The Message for Today

If the Alchemist has come to you today you are being asked to see beyond the story that is erupting into your consciousness right now and discover the keys of transformation and healing held sacred within the story. There is healing to be done.

34

Observer

The Observer is the Wise Woman who sees the whole picture rather than fragments of the story. She stands quietly on the periphery and sees the truth. She also works with the Truth Seeker to see what is real and what is false.

The Observer will point out the truth she sees when needed. She is a good mediator. She is a keen observer of human nature. She is also a keen observer of nature's cycles and will do well seeking her wisdom from the cycles of life. Her understanding of cycles from clear observation will see patterns emerge for the journey of those who seek her and also for the greater community and world.

The Observer will do well with pursuits in astrology or numerology. Being a keen observer will see her putting the patterns that emerge in these pursuits together with what she observes in humanity.

The Observer will want to right the world or at least demonstrate to others how they can journey well if they follow the patterns in the stars, numbers or perhaps in some other field of interest.

The Ancient Ones have honoured the Observer with the gift of keen observation and perception of how the patterns of life and pieces fit together to create a bigger picture.

The Message for Today

If the Observer has come to you today you are being asked to look at the patterns emerging within your own life. There is change happening for you and around you. The patterns you see as the Observer will assist you to create a detour from your current path.

35

Gardener

The Gardener will always tend to the gardens of life, her own and others. With her hands in the earth she brings forward the wisdom of Mother Earth, the Spirit of the Goddess. She sees the beauty and potential of empty spaces. She is also the Seer, able to see beyond the blank canvas presented to her, to tend and grow.

The Gardener loves colour and surrounding herself with flowers of many different hues. She loves to grow vegetables and fruits to harvest. The Gardener will work with herbs for healing and wellbeing. She is aware that what you seed and nourish, will in time, be ready for harvest. She works with this as a metaphor for her own life and in helping others to tend their own inner gardens.

The Gardener loves the balance of tending the garden for joy and tending it for nourishment and healing. She loves to be out in nature. This is where she feels most alive and where she receives the wisdom she shares as a Wise Woman of the earth. In tending the gardens of life, healing flows through all of the earth.

The Gardener knows her way is to show others how to tend their own gardens, physically and metaphorically, with tender care.

The Ancient Ones have honoured the Gardener with the gift of earth healing through beautiful colours and fragrances and soul nourishment.

The Message for Today:

If the Gardener has come to you today you are being asked to tend your garden with love and care. Pull the weeds which represent healing the old stories. Till the soil to freshen the journey. Add organic matter, which is the decay of old outworn ways of being, in order to fertilise the soil ready for planting. Plant new seeds and nurture them to grow a new chapter in your life story. You are ready for the next step on life's journey.

36

Priestess

The Priestess will hold the journey of life in the highest regard. She will be the one who in initiates ritual on a daily basis and work with ceremony in order to set foundations for the new. She is the Keeper of Mysteries of the Ancient Rites. The moon and the dark of the night holds considerable power in her world.

She is feminine, powerful and strong. The Priestess knows she holds the keys to empowerment through sacred ritual and ceremony. It might be as simple as a tea ceremony or a deeper earth-based ritual involving the moon in her different phases.

She is love. She shares her deep wisdom and knowledge with those who seek out the Divine Feminine, the sacred Goddess within. The Priestess came into this world with a knowing beyond what is taught. She is now weaving her ritualistic magic to create more balance in this changing world.

The Priestess knows her role is to offer sacred ritual and ceremony as an alternative to the mundane, in order to create change within life.

The Ancient Ones have honoured the Priestess with the gift of beauty that shines from within. There is an air of magic around her that is revealed to those who seek her company and wisdom.

The Message for Today

If the Priestess has come to you today you are being asked to honour your own journey in a ritualistic way. Light a sacred fire and divine the messages held within the flames. Write and say out loud some sacred prayers. Sing or drum. You are preparing to step into a more sacred way of being in charge of your own destiny. Ritual and ceremony will show you the way.

37
❦

Earth Angel

The Earth Angel feels the pain of the world immensely. She can be also an Empath, but her journey is one of helping those who seek her. Her solutions are of the highest spiritual order. She knows the higher reasons of the world. Her compassion is strong but so is her will. What others see as vulnerability is actually her strength to just be true to her journey, without concerning herself with the expectations of others.

She can be easily hurt and not understand the ways of this human world. The Earth Angel has a light that is beyond this world and yet others cannot put what they see and feel into words. She has an enigmatic smile because she knows the truth beyond the words spoken. Her presence often changes the energy of the room without others being aware of why they feel good or different.

She often seems to be in the right place at the right time. She honours truth above all else. She knows she is here to awaken humanity to the destruction they place on one another, on animals and the earth herself. The physical world is a conundrum to the Earth Angel but she keeps working towards educating others on better ways of experiencing life.

The Earth Angel knows there is a better way and that her role in life is to share her knowledge.

The Ancient Ones have honoured the Earth Angel with the gift of helping others see a better way. The key is to know that not all will listen but many will be given pause for thought.

The Message for Today

If the Earth Angel has come to you today you are being asked to look within to see what is true for you. To look deeply at something within your life that will be honoured by truthful communication.

38

Witch

The Witch has an ability to work with the elements to weave her magic in life. She is often misunderstood and perhaps ridiculed for her witchy ways and yet the natural order of the world is paramount to her Witch persona and work. She will like creating in her kitchen. Everything from food to potions for the wellbeing of the mind, body and soul. Her garden may be overgrown but the Witch will have important herbs, flowers and vegetables growing in places most others wouldn't think of seeding.

The Witch is a keeper of secret lore, sharing with those who seek something for the journey. It could be wisdom or something more tangible such as a herbal remedy or perhaps as ordinary as a cake.

She will write incantations and spells or create recipes to tantalise the seeker. Her way is many ways and all lead down a healing/healer pathway. The Witch in her everyday life will not always be apparent to the ordinary person. Those who resonate with earth medicine will find her easily when the time is right.

The Witch knows her path is one of working with the earth and the elements of nature to affect powerful change in the world.

The Ancient Ones have honoured the Witch with the gift of putting her hands in the earth to understand the work of the Goddess as she creates sacred gifts for those who seek her ways.

The Message for Today

If the Witch has come to you today you are being asked to dig in your garden and get your hands dirty. Feel your connection to the Goddess and the Witch within you. You are awakening an ancient path and it is time to walk it with pride. Your creative spirit is ready to head into the garden and into the kitchen to create beautiful magic.

39

Gatherer

The Gatherer hunts for knowledge, often in the unlikeliest of places. She communicates with the natural world so that she is guided to where she needs to be to gather information for the journey.

She carries her basket—which represents the womb of creation—to gather wisdom and knowledge. She gathers anything from stones to plants to feathers. Often the unusual finds its way to her. Each gift from nature is a messenger to the Gatherer.

She has the gift of arrangement, creating beautiful offerings that draw the eye and heart of those who seek her. Each arrangement is a sacred story that speaks to the heart of the matter presenting itself. Each creation holds sacred meaning to both the Gatherer and the one who loves it. The Gatherer loves to gift the offerings to others who are drawn to them.

She knows most of what she gathers is not for her to keep. It will find its way to the one who needs it, no matter how long it takes. The receiver of the gift will connect to and understand the message.

The Gatherer is aware of all of nature and as she walks or forages she will discover special gifts for creating and gifting to others.

The Ancient Ones have honoured the Gatherer with the gift of gathering wisdom and knowledge of the earth through each element found in nature. She has the ability to see beyond an ordinary stone or deep within the most beautiful flower to reach for the messages inherent within the gift. Such is the nature of the Gatherer.

The Message for Today

If the Gatherer has come to you today you are being asked to walk in nature and collect offerings that call

to you. You are being asked to open your heart and listen to the messages that come. Build a sacred story with your gifts.

40

Seeker

The Seeker always desires more knowledge about life. She knows that the more she seeks, the more she will find the answers she needs to help herself and others. The Seeker likes to uncover life's mysteries and share them. Her discoveries lead others to seek her to find out more about their world.

She is drawn to scientific views with a spiritual overlay as she seeks to understand the world and the Universe from many different angles. She is willing to learn from others and from life and nature as she embarks on her Seeker journey.

She will often be drawn to travel to obscure places to find the meaning of life, to seek her answers within something more than what appears on the surface. The Seeker has a sharp mind and can absorb both knowledge and energy in order to find balance within what she seeks.

Often her search brings more questions than answers. In time the answers come. Often just when she thought the search was done.

The Seeker is aware that all knowledge is available within nature. Her gift affords her the ability to look beyond what *appears* to be real, to the depth of what it is she is seeking.

The Ancient Ones have honoured the Seeker with the gift of an intellect that seeks the deeper wisdom and knowledge found in the natural world. When she discovers something important, the Seeker knows that she needs to share that wisdom and knowledge with others.

The Message for Today

If the Seeker has come to you today you are being asked to look deeper into a situation to discover the truth. Someone close to you will seek your wisdom and knowledge. Or perhaps you are seeking deeper knowledge in a

situation for personal reasons. You have the ability now to use your seeker magic to discover truth and weave it into a new story.

41

Crystal Guardian

The Crystal Guardian will know when a crystal is ready to speak with her. Crystals will come to her in dreams, visions and in unusual ways. The Crystal Guardian is aware that she is a guardian rather than a keeper of crystals. She will always know when to gift her crystals to those who need their inherent power, wisdom and healing.

Crystals hold the knowledge and wisdom of not only this planet but the Universe. The Crystal Guardian will deepen her understanding of what the crystal means through her meditative practices which allow the crystal to take her on a journey into its heart. The Crystal Guardian has the ability to also be the Seer and read for others by 'throwing' the crystals and reading their symbolic messages. She is often self-taught and will seek others who hold knowledge of the crystals to learn more.

The Crystal Guardian will often discover that one special crystal will find her and be with her throughout her journey. It may arrive as a gift or perhaps she will be drawn to a space that sells crystals because she has heard the call of her crystal. This crystal will be her guide on her journey.

The Crystal Guardian is aware that crystals can do nothing by themselves. Her work comes from awakening others to the wisdom and knowledge of the crystal kingdom and this includes the stones of the earth.

The Ancient Ones have honoured the Crystal Guardian with the gift of instruction in the way of the crystals. Her crystal knowledge is full of love, joy, innocence and power and was seeded long before her incarnation to this earth.

The Message for Today

If the Crystal Guardian has come to you today you are being asked to seek a special crystal to aid your journey now. You are being asked to look deep within the crystalline structures of your own body to see what requires healing in mind, body or soul. You may also be asked to help another on their journey by offering the gift of a crystal as a tangible reminder that they are loved.

42

Moon Goddess

The Moon Goddess understands that she is of the earth but she also resonates with the moon and her cycles. The Moon Goddess loves the power of ritual and ceremony to honour these different cycles. She loves to offer others the opportunity to embrace the moon in her different phases.

The Moon Goddess is energised on the full of the moon as it illuminates aspects of life to be examined and perhaps healed or as an honouring of her powerful cycle. She understands the need to journey within the dark of the moon as she sows new seeds for the next cycle, a powerful Wise Woman time just before the arrival of the new moon. She is also the Gardener tending her inner and outer garden by the cycles of the moon.

The feminine nature of the Moon Goddess is strong. The pull of the energies often makes her an Empath, a woman sensitive to the nature of others seeking their own journey in life. There is a need to protect her sensitive nature so that she may work with the different powerful phases of the moon.

The Moon Goddess needs to keep her feet firmly on the ground to notice what is happening around her and see those who are seeking her. However, it is the night sky connecting with the moon that is her realm of understanding. This is where she blends the wisdom of the earth with the moon energy, in order to teach others who intuitively know the moon is their way of perceiving life's journey.

As the Moon Goddess she is aware that her journey is one of cycles, particularly the moon cycles. She understands that the moon's influence on her own life will overflow to others who feel that same pull of feminine energy.

The Ancient Ones have honoured the Moon Goddess with the gift of working with women and their cycles through understanding the cycles of the moon and their own personal power times. The gift is one of deep intuitive femininity and one to be honoured is this sacred way.

The Message for Today

If the Moon Goddess has come to you today you are being asked to look to your own cycles to understand what needs to be brought back into balance in your life. Are your quests for something new out of balance with the cycles of the moon? Use your intuition to guide yourself back onto the right trail for optimal success.

43

Ceremonial Wise Woman

The Ceremonial Wise Woman works with ceremony as an integral part of her life. She honours all life and her place in it. Each morning on waking she honours the day with her intentions. The Ceremonial Wise Woman knows the value of her sacred intentions.

As she goes about her day her actions are a deliberate reflection of what she has set for herself for the day ahead. When those intentions are disrupted, she will step back and be the Observer. She will then calmly alter her course to find a better way to achieve those intentions. If, at the end of the day they have not come to fruition she surrenders them as tomorrow is another day waiting to set new intentions.

Life is a ceremony of intentions for this Wise Woman. The Ceremonial Wise Woman will teach others who seek her, how to live life in sacred ceremony. She will share her way of creating success in life.

As the Ceremonial Wise Woman, she is also the Story Weaver, sharing her stories of life's journey. She shares her wisdom about how to let go of the old stories and weave a new story with ceremony. Her journey is powerful but fuelled by inner wisdom and contentment.

The Ceremonial Wise Woman is aware that she has a powerful message to share through the beauty of ceremony. It is like a song sung from the heart of want and need, setting creative intention through ceremonial ways to achieve everyday success in everyday life. Ceremony keeps her focus strong.

The Ancient Ones have honoured the Ceremonial Wise Woman with the innate gift of knowing ceremony, of tapping into ancient ways to create the life she wants and needs; held within the seeds of light she brought with her into this world. With this knowledge she will encourage others who seek her to work with daily ceremony to create within their own lives.

The Message for Today

If the Ceremonial Wise Woman has come to you today you are being asked to open yourself to sacred ceremony to set new intentions for your daily life. There is a goal you are wanting to achieve and sacred ceremony and setting clear intentions will be part of your journey. Ceremony can be as simple or as complex as you wish. Write your own and begin to create change in an area of your life today.

44

Writer

The Writer works deeply with her inner creative spirit. Her written words carry a vibration that touches the hearts and souls of those who read them. It is her loving intention as she writes that reaches those hearts who need her words.

It is also her own words, that come directly as a message from her inner Wise Woman, that will guide her own life. The Writer creates stories from her heart. Words have the ability to lift someone's day; their life. The Writer will express herself in ways others cannot. Her writings are full of love, emotion and power.

When the Writer sets out to share her creative spirit through her words, she sets an intention to provoke deep thought and even deeper feelings. As the Writer, this Wise Woman may sometimes need a tough armour to protect her expressions from those who fail to understand her intent. The Writer has the ability to paint a picture with her words. Others who resonate with her words will seek her wisdom to learn how to express themselves with beautiful intent in their own lives.

The Writer will show others how to write a new chapter within their own life story. It is by living by her own expressions that she will lead others to do the same.

The Writer is aware of the power held within her expressions. She takes her creative ability seriously and works with this sacred tool for the empowerment of those who read her words.

The Ancient Ones have honoured the Writer with the innate gift of creative writing. Her words are a gift to share with others who read them. They have offered this gift, this beautiful way of expression to the Writer as a way to reach many. The written word holds a high vibration when it is gifted in light.

The Message for Today

If the Writer has come to you today you are being asked to express yourself with words. Write a letter to express your feelings of pain, of love, of forgiveness about an old story coming to the surface of your consciousness. When you feel you have written all you need to, create a sacred ritual to burn your letter so that your heartfelt feelings are carried on the smoke energetically to where they need to go, in order to be released in a powerful way, with love.

45

Elemental Guardian

The Elemental Guardian is a protector of nature. She communicates with the elemental beings that live in her garden and in the wider world. Nature is her sanctuary. The Elemental Guardian sees beyond the ordinary into the extraordinary world of the fairies, devas and nature spirits. The world of fire, earth, air and water spirits.

As the Elemental Guardian she is also the Gardener and the Seer. Her own garden will often be light and bright as she honours those elementals who live there.

The Elemental Guardian will help protect waterways and forests to the best of her ability. She will be a voice for the elementals and she will encourage others who seek her to also be guardians.

When the Elemental Guardian does not have a physical garden of her own, she knows her inner garden will offer sanctuary. Those who seek the wisdom of the Elemental Guardian will find themselves working alongside her with their hands in the earth. A vegetable garden, herbs perhaps, digging weeds or companion planting. Listening to the Elemental Guardian's stories of nature and how they may relate to life experiences will enrich the journey.

The Elemental Guardian is aware of the need to be in nature to discover the wisdom of the plants, the sky, the moon and the elemental beings and how everything links together.

The Ancient Ones have honoured the Elemental Guardian with the innate gift of knowing plants and their sacred elemental signature. The Elemental Guardian's gift is one of understanding the messages that come from the physical world through the elemental beings in the form of birds, animals and insects as well as seeing beyond ordinary sight and into the world of the magical.

The Message for Today

If the Elemental Guardian has come to you today you are being asked to step outside and connect with nature as there is a message for you to know. Walking mindfully in nature and opening your awareness to what exists beyond the ordinary will see vibrancy be a part of your day. There is a new exciting trail for you to follow, within and without.

46

Free Spirit

The Free Spirit loves to spread her wings and fly in the face of convention. She cannot be confined by the rules of others. Her spirit is restless when she feels contained. She longs to break free and usually does.

The Free Spirit is love. She emits love like a beacon from the soul of her being. She is a woman who also embodies the Seer. She has the ability to see beyond the ordinary and into the extraordinary. Her world is full of light and song and dancing. She is never still, wanting to experience life to the best of her ability, even if at times it is only experienced from the inner realms. This will settle her spirit for a while but she will soon be looking for the next adventure.

Others are drawn to her so that they too may experience the adventure. She is also a Story Weaver, weaving her sacred stories into something exciting for others to hear.

The Free Spirit is self-aware. She knows her vulnerabilities and limitations but more importantly she knows her strengths. Over her lifetime the Free Spirit learns to work with whatever tools will help her fly high. She may not stay for long in one place although her heart and thoughts will leave an indelible mark on where she has been.

The Free Spirit is aware of her need to show others how to spread their own wings. She is a leader who leads by example. She encourages women not to follow her blindly, instead showing them how to free their spirit in order to soar.

The Ancient Ones have honoured the Free Spirit with the gift of loving life without restriction and sharing that love with others who seek her so that they too may understand the need to fly high.

The Message for Today

If the Free Spirit has come to you today you are being asked to stand guard against any restrictive behaviours you may be exhibiting. Your soul longs to fly, to experience something new. It is time to embrace a new adventure. Who will help you fly high now?

47

Keeper of the Flame

The Keeper of the Flame has a passion for life that others may not understand. The flame of life burns brightly within her. She is also the Healer and will assist others on their healing journey with the sacredness of fire.

The Keeper of the Flame will see things in the torchlight that will make perfect sense to her. Flames dance for her. She sees the elementals dancing in the beauty of its light. Others are drawn to the Keeper of the Flame because they see her passion and her light burning brightly. She needs to learn discernment so that she does not burn out from those who seek to put out her flame.

Many will feel the call of the Keeper of the Flame long before they meet. She is everything from a candle flame to a bonfire. She must learn how to control the flames so they do not burn her or others.

She is a master of ceremony, knowing how to keep the soul fires burning. Her way is not for the faint hearted as it is full of passion and fiery energy. The Keeper of the Flame is often a wonderful creatrix in her world, creating her desires and needs through hard work and intuition. She is a warrior woman who fights for all she believes in. She speaks her truth clearly and eloquently. She is a powerful motivator for those who seek her fiery ways.

The Keeper of the Flame is aware that her role in life is to make things happen in the right way to obtain the best results. She knows that she cannot shy away from her destiny and that her voice is one to be heard clearly. She is one of the leaders of change.

The Ancient Ones have honoured the Keeper of the Flame with the dual gifts of passion and a vibrant spirit. These gifts will touch those who seek her light with a passion for life and the opportunity to live life to its fullest potential.

The Message for Today

If the Keeper of the Flame has come to you today you are being asked to ignite a new project. Something needs the input of your vibrant and passionate energy in order to succeed. Perhaps there is a project you have cast aside for a while. There is a need to reignite your drive and passion to move it forward. A relationship may need some extra fire right now.

48

Spirit of the Goddess

The Spirit of the Goddess is the embodiment of Mother Earth. She is strong, vulnerable, proud, courageous, gentle and loving, depending on what is needed at a given time in her life. The Spirit of the Goddess is a nurturer but in a way that embraces tough love at times.

She knows things that many others do not, however, she prefers to only share what she knows, at the right time and to the right person. She is connected to nature and sees the beauty in all of the natural world.

The Spirit of the Goddess is Divinely Feminine. This succulent woman exudes a sacred sensuality that is like honey to a bee. She is the Mother, the Wise Woman, the Crone, the Maiden. She is all of these things and yet none, seeking instead to show her unique nature. She is like a chameleon who can be one thing to one person who seeks her wisdom and something different to another. Such is the beauty of the Spirit of the Goddess.

She is the teacher of the old ways of connecting with the earth to bring about solid change so she will guide others well. The Spirit of the Goddess knows how to stand her ground in her own feminine way. When she knows she is right nothing will shake her resolve. She speaks gently but powerfully. She knows that her way, is the way to create a better future for those who travel this journey behind her. She is a leader who often works behind the scenes, showing up to do her work and offering guidance when asked about how to navigate the trails ahead.

The Spirit of the Goddess is aware of her feminine spirit and just how powerful that femininity can be when put into action. She knows that those who seek her are awake to the ways of the Goddess and that they are looking for her guidance to find the best trail to follow in life.

The Ancient Ones have honoured the Spirit of the Goddess with the gift of connection with the great Goddess, Mother Earth. Her gifts are to show others how to connect and know grace, humility, love and nurturance through the ancient ways.

The Message for Today

If the Spirit of the Goddess has come to you today you are being asked to connect with the Goddess within and seek your own inner wisdom. There is a message available to you as you connect with the Goddess, Mother Earth. You are being called to learn the ancient ways and ultimately share these ways with others who seek you. You are being asked to ignite your innately sensual nature and stand in your Divine Feminine power.

Ceremony to Invoke the Wise Woman

The Wise Woman is available to women of all ages. She is available to all men who wish to tap into the Wise Woman as their guide. She is that innate inner wise guide who has stories to share and who will offer different roads of self-discovery. This mini ceremony is to assist you in invoking the innate Wise Woman within you and to also be open to welcoming more Wise Women into your life.

The more that the Wise Woman remembers her journey and the more that men also remember they have this inner wise guide walking with them, the more the Wise Woman will connect with others to create change in this world. This is a journey based in love.

I love to connect with the Wise Woman in nature however weather or circumstances may require you to perform ceremony inside.

What You Will Need

- Clear quartz crystal to amplify the energies.
- Firepit if you are working outdoors. Set your fire ready to light prior to performing ceremony.
- Candle in a safe receptacle if you are working indoors. Intuitively choose a colour or natural candle that feels right to you.
- Sage or other cleansing herbs and a fireproof receptacle to safely cleanse your space.
- Matches or a lighter.
- A special place where you will not be disturbed.
- A copy of this ceremony.
- Ambient music if you are working indoors or listen to the sounds of nature if you are outdoors.
- Stones, crystals or shells to create a circle around you to contain the energy as you perform your ceremony. Your circle can be created with anything at all. For example,

leaves if you are in nature. Let your imagination be your guide. As you collect your tools to create ceremony you are already feeling the pull of the Wise Woman within you.

Ceremony

This is a sacred ceremony for you to welcome your inner Wise Woman or your inner Wise Woman guide. You are walking a road of remembering who you are as you journey towards a sacred place within, hearing the powerful call of the Wise Woman.

When you intuitively know where you would like to perform ceremony, create your sacred circle. Make it big enough to sit in. Leave an opening in the east in which to enter.

Gather your clear quartz crystal, your herbs to cleanse your space and receptacle and matches. If you are inside begin to set the intention by turning on your ambient music and place your unlit candle in its receptacle in the centre of your circle. You are ready to begin.

Enter your sacred circle in the east and move sunwise all the way around the circle before finding the direction in which you would like to sit. Place your crystal in the centre of your circle alongside your candle or firepit. Close the door of the east with a crystal or other item with which you created your circle. You have now set your intention for the power of your personal ceremony to build. You are well protected within your sacred sanctuary.

Return to your position within the circle and light your candle or fire and welcome the sacred flame as the opening of this ceremony. You will begin to feel the palpable energy shift as it is contained within this sacred space. Only good will come to you here today.

Light your sacred herbs in their safe receptacle. Walk sunwise around your circle cleansing your space saying a small prayer. Do the same over and around your body. For example, you might like to say,

> I willingly release anything that is not energetically
> compatible with my intention to meet my inner
> Wise Woman today.

When you have finished, place the receptacle on the ground near your candle or fire and allow it to extinguish by itself.

Your quartz crystal is amplifying the beautiful energies present in your ceremony, reflecting your intention to welcome your Wise Woman. The power of your sacred space is intensifying with the power of love.

Sit quietly in your sacred space for a few moments feeling the building of these loving powerful energies.

When you are ready, invoke the Wise Woman within you with the following invocation. Speak it out loud in a sing song way.

> I call on the Wise Woman
> to come to me now.
> I seek your wise words
> And make this sacred vow.
> I listen with my heart
> To what you willingly share
> The Wise Woman in me
> Acknowledges your ancient care.
> I am the Wise Woman
> Vibrant and heard
> I am powerful and strong
> Now the Wise Woman has stirred.
> I call on your beauty
> Your courage and light
> The Wise Woman remembered
> Is now in plain sight.
> The seeds are sown
> For a new way to be
> The Wise Woman in me
> Is there for *all* to see.

Take some time to allow the Wise Woman in you to emerge into your life. Feel her presence within this sacred circle. Once she is invoked, she will be with you whenever you need her to work with you.

Ask your Wise Woman for any messages to guide you on your journey forward. Take some time to sit in this space and listen with your heart as you open your senses to the messages of the Wise Woman.

It is time to close your ceremony.

You will begin to feel the energy of your ceremony dissipate. Share some of this beautiful energy you have experienced with the Goddess, Mother Earth. Extinguish your candle or allow your fire to burn out naturally if it is safe to do so. Gather your crystal and any other tools you worked with in ceremony and move around your circle in the opposite direction to how you entered, towards the gateway in the east. Open the gateway to your circle and turn to offer gratitude for your ceremony and this time of invoking the spirit of the Wise Woman.

You may choose to leave the circle in place or dismantle it, putting away the sacred tools until the next time you want to perform ceremony. Celebrate your ceremony and your connection with the Wise Woman by doing something you love, to honour you and your journey.

Suggestions for honouring the Wise Woman beyond ceremony:

- Carry your clear quartz crystal with you or work with it to welcome the Wise Woman in your magical workings. This crystal will be a tangible reminder of the spirit of the Wise Woman in your life.
- Paint or draw your Wise Woman.
- Meditate with her whenever you need her.
- Create a special place or garden in which to sit in quiet contemplation with the Wise Woman.

For all the beautiful women who are ready to embrace their Wise Woman, enjoy the journey!

With love

Jude

Jude Downes is a story-weaver of metaphoric stories for healing and life's journey. She is an author, a Clairvoyant and an Intuitive Mentor with certificates in Psycho Spiritual Hypnotherapy, Colour Therapy and Reiki. Jude's healing words work with metaphors through the power of story to affect deep and lasting transformation. She is passionate about helping others on their life journey.

Jude is a 'Healer with Words'. She encourages people to write a new chapter in their personal life story. She is the creator of sacred workshops and retreats. Her intimate connection to The Goddess ~ the Earth Mother and the messages that come from nature weave a path in the unity between mind, body, soul and emotions to form the foundations of her business, Dreaming the Seed.

www.judedownes.com

Other titles by Jude Downes

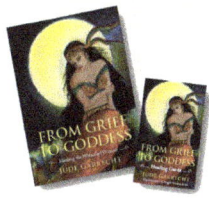

From Grief to Goddess Book and Healing Cards
2014 self-published by Jude Downes and Animal Dreaming Publishing

Gateway to the Modern Crone
2019 self-published by Jude Downes and Adala Publishing

The Story of Woman
The Mountain
Book One
2019 self-published by Jude Downes and Adala Publishing

www.ingramcontent.com/pod-product-compliance
Lightning Source LLC
Chambersburg PA
CBHW062059290426
44110CB00022B/2646